I0099468

The Time is Now:

Things Stolen to Be Restored

By Dr. Janice Robinson

TRUE PERSPECTIVE PUBLISHING HOUSE

Autograph Page

**Dedicate this book to someone who
is in the process of restoration**

AKNOWLEDGEMENTS AND DEDICATIONS

I dedicate this book to my prayer partners, Christian Manna Outreach Inc., the Women and Men Of Purpose, Pastor Estelle Lynch, Pastor Thomas Lynch and Evangelist Diane Williams.

Our nonprofit Ministry outreaches to help the hurting, the needy through Ministry, Evangelism, conferences and food drive. Through our ministry we have witnessed healing, miracles, families being restored, and salvation for our brother's and sister's. We have also, experienced many
testimonies from people who have attended our conferences over the many years here in Clermont Florida.

To my Pastor, Bishop, Chris Dutruch, his wife, Julie Dutruch and family for their dedication to bring the word of God through teaching the Bible and applying it to our lives on a daily basis. May God bless you, Bishop Chris and family!

To my sons Tory Robinson, Jonathan Robinson. My sisters, brothers and their families. Associate

Minster Mary Robinson, Dorothy World, Lois Callaway, Shirley Robinson, George Robinson and to my mother,

the late, Rosa Lee Robinson and my two siblings, the late, Helen Motley, Robert Robinson and Jackie Robinson. To my late Grandparents, Rev. and Mrs. Willie Allen of Norman, Fla. And to my late aunt, Claudia Allen. Along with a host of nieces, nephews, uncles, cousins and grandchildren.

To my friend Iris Figueroa and her husband Nelson Figueroa who has believed in me through the writing of my book.

May the words in this book inspire you to read your Bible more, to pray more and ask God to bring revelation and understanding to your mind and your thoughts. May the word of God bring peace, life and joy to your understanding.

TABLE OF CONTENTS

PREFACE

The Time is Now! God is sending healing to His people and restoring everything that has been stolen from their lives and from the lives of their children. We must believe that God's word does not lie but speaks truth and that we the believers will accomplish much by what the Word of God has sent us out to do. As you read this book my prayer is that God will open up your understanding and teach you through His word the things to come into this world. "He that hath an ear, let him hear what the spirit saith unto the churches. (Revelation 2:17)"[1] Our God is restoring everything back to His people! He is also restoring our children and our family members back to Him.

These are times that we all need to come back together as a family and allow God to restore His love back into the hearts of those who believe in Him. "And I will restore to you the years that the locust hath eaten, the cankerworm, and the caterpillar, and the palmerworm my great army which I sent among you. And ye shall eat in plenty and He shall satisfy, and praise the name of the Lord your God, that hath dealt wondrously with you and my people shall never be ashamed. And ye shall know that I am in the midst of Israel and that I am the Lord your God, and none else: and my people shall never be ashamed. (Joel 2:25-27)"[1]

It is encouraging to continue to hear what the Lord is saying in these times and seasons. I thought it was only going to be one book that I was going to write but God knows everything that is going to take place in our lives. I feel like this is going to be a series of books that God wants me to write and allow the readers to hear what the Lord is saying. God is always speaking to us but we have to be quiet and listen for his voice and obey His word.

CHAPTER 1

Our Lord is restoring everything that the enemy has stolen from our lives! He is bringing our families back together to rule in this world and when families are together, believing on one thing, it is a powerful tool. God is restoring His children! When we come together as a family and spend time with God, we can expect to see the blessing of God begin to operate in our lives.

This is a choice that we have to make in order to show God that we love him; we want to serve him and do all that He has ordained for us, His sons and daughters to do upon this earth.

We as God's children have many blessings that will come into our lives, however we need to learn to worship God and praise him for who He is and what he has done for his children. He honors our praise when we glorify His name in the earth. When we do this God can inhabit our praise and come into the midst of our problems, situations and work them out. As His sons and daughters we must believe that our Father can overturn our problems and turn them around for His glory.

God will restore everything that the enemy has stolen from us and use us to bring in the harvest of souls for His kingdom. God is moving by His spirit in the earth today to shake everything that can be shaken in the earth this hour, to accomplish His plans for all of His children. This is the season for us to carry out God's plan in the earth to win the lost at any cost! He is not just restoring blessings to lavish on ourselves but to help others who are in need and especially those who desperately need the word of God to enrich their lives.

This is a season of hope and prosperity for all of us who will take God at His word and praise Him with our mouth, heart and soul.

He knows who He can trust to carry out His plans to change the lives and the hearts of His people. "For in these days, saith God, there is a divine increase of prosperity coming to my people. My promise to you is to prosper you not to harm you.

As you hear my voice, saith the Lord, and act upon my words, I will fulfill my words in your life, for didn't I say that the wealth of the wicked is laid up for the righteous?

Didn't I say that you will eat the good and the fat of the land if you are willing and obedient? Didn't I say that I have prepared a table for you in the presence of your enemies? (Proverbs 13:22)"[1] Believe God's Word and His promises and you will inherit the riches of His kingdom.

To those who believe are a light in the darkest night! And it is a very dark world that we are living in but the Lord said, "My light will shine on those who believe, saith the Lord, I will send wisdom, knowledge and my anointing, blessing and prosperity upon my people to prosper and give them divine favor. This is the day for all your possessions that were lost are restored to you.

But thou shall remember the Lord thy God: For it is he that giveth thee power to get wealth that he may establish his covenant which he swear unto thy fathers, as it is this day. (Deuteronomy 8:18)"[1]
In this season of increase and prosperity God's anointing shall be poured out upon His people and the hand of God will bless His people in due season.

"Thou shalt fear the Lord thy God; Him shalt thou serve, and to Him shalt thou cleave, and swear by His name. (Deuteronomy 10:20)"[1] We should remember always to serve others who are in need and who suffer in lack and have a poor spirit of knowledge in the word of God. For in these days, God will give you peace, rest, joy and relaxation from your works. This is your time of jubilee, "saith the Lord thy God bringeth thee into a good land, a land of brooks of water, of fountains and depth that spring out of valleys and hills; A land of wheat, and barley, and vines and fig trees, and pomegranates; a land of olive oil, and honey; A land wherein thou shall eat bread   without scarceness thou shalt not lack any thing in it: a land whose stones are iron, and out of whose hills thou may dig brass. (Deuteronomy 8:7-9)"[1]

Chapter 2

*G*od is restoring land and possessions back into the hands of His people who will keep His Commandments and walk in his ways, those who will fear him with a holy reverence. "For my tithe is holy seed and as you sow my holy seed into the work of my kingdom so that there will be food in my house for my children, I will cause the windows of heaven to be opened wide above you so that my blessings may flow fully into your life and at the same time the devourer will be rebuked. (Deuteronomy 8:8-9)"[1]

When we obey God's command He can give us instruction on how to follow His plans and the way we should go, not our own. As we continue to act upon the word of God, He will guide us and show us miracles that have never happened before in our lifetime.

Our Lord is restoring our land and our possessions back to his people as their inheritance. "The Lord is the portion of mine inheritance and of my cup: thou maintain my lot. Therefore, we have confidence in our Lord that he delights in us as his children who rejoices and is hopeful in our God. (Psalm 1:5-6)"[1]

As we continue to show our confidence in God for our land and possessions to be returned back to us, we should never forget how Jesus paved the way for us through His suffering on the cross and the shedding of His blood for our sins, our sickness and our diseases. We serve a mighty God and his words are truth, mighty and powerful.

As we read God's word in the bible, we must believe that whatever he says will come to pass in our lives if we believe and meditate on His words.

Jesus said pray, believe and whatever we ask for in His name it shall be given unto us. He already sees the need in our lives before we even speak and He knows if we will take Him at His word.

God hears our problems and knows our desires as we bring them to lay down at His feet. When we lay our problems down we must not worry but wait on God, He is always there when we need Him most. He is an on time God! Many times in my own life and my struggles God has showed up just at the right time for me and my family. I can remember when we needed a place to live and we only had days to find a house here in Florida. God moved in our situation and showed up on time. He said I will restore your land unto you and your children for an inheritance.

"That thou may go in unto the land which the Lord thy God giveth thee, a land that floweth with milk and honey: as the Lord God of thy fathers hath promised thee. (Deuteronomy 27:3)"[1]

Chapter 3

*N*ow is the time to increase our faith and believe God for our bodies to be healed, to accomplish the work that He has for us to do in the ministry. "You have forgiven all my iniquities; you have healed all my diseases; You have redeemed my life from destruction; you have satisfied my mouth with good things so that my youth is renewed as the eagles. (Psalms 103:2-5)"[1] God wants His people to be healthy and eat the right foods for the benefit of their good health.

He also wants His people to stop worrying and being stressed of things that they can't handle but to put everything in His hands. God is healing, strengthening our bodies and making us whole again and allowing us to be prosperous and have everything we need and more!

Our Father through our faith is restoring many, supernaturally all around the world by just hearing His word. Through our faith is where our healing begins and as we believe our bodies can be restored, healing will come upon us. "When he had thus spoken He spat on the spittle, and He anointed the eyes of the blind man with the clay, And said unto him, Go, wash in the pool of Silo-am, He went his way therefore, and washed, and came seeing. (John 9:6-7)"[1] He is a healer.

If our body is broken and tired, we will not be able to carry out our mission to minister to the world. He is reversing the sickness and diseases off of us! When we believe He is the Christ and that He is alive sitting on the right hand of the Father, the word says, "ask for what you need and it shall be done."[1] We must believe that God will heal our bodies if we believe by faith.

When we read our Bibles and focus on the foods that we should eat, our bodies will function as God has instructed it to be.
We need to speak the word!

"There is one who speaks like the piercing of a sword: but the tongue of the wise promotes health (Proverbs 12:18)"[1]

Now, is the time for us to declare healing over us! We should speak this over our bodies each and every day: Body, I speak the word of faith to you. I demand that every internal organ perform a perfect work, for you are the temple of the Holy Ghost; Therefore, I charge you in the name of the Lord Jesus Christ and by the Authority of His holy word to be healed and made whole in Jesus' name.

As we meditate on the word of God it will help us grow, learn and not allow sin, sickness or death to lord over our lives. As children of God we have to change our lifestyle, go back to the Bible, focus on His word and live life to the fullest. There are many people in the Bible that have lived to a very old age like Abraham and Sara. God wants us to live a long healthy life! "For verily, I say unto you, that whosoever shall say unto this mountain be thou removed and be thou cast into the sea and shall not doubt in his heart but shall believe that those things which he says shall come to pass; he shall have whatsoever he saith. (Mark 11:23)"[1] Declare, My immune system grows stronger day by day. I speak life to my immune system. I forbid confusion in my immune system. The same spirit that raised Christ from the dead dwells in me and quickens my immune system with life from the word of God, which guards the life and health of my body in Jesus name.[2]

Chapter 4

*G*od is restoring His children back to their parents. He said, "He will pour out His spirit upon His children in the last days. (Joel 2:28)"[1] He is turning the hearts of his children back to the Father. And God will send His peace upon your children, they shall learn to hear the voice of the Lord. Isaiah 54:13 says, "And all thy children shall be taught of the Lord; and great shall be the peace of thy children."[1]

The enemy has no authority over the lives of our children! "No weapon that is formed against thee shall prosper: and every tongue that shall rise against thee in judgment thou shalt condemn. This is the heritage of the servants of the Lord, and their righteousness is of me, saith the Lord. (Isaiah 54:17)"[1]

As parents we should teach our children about the Bible and make it a daily part of your family life. As your children learn the word of God it will bring your family closer together.

When families pray together this strengthens the family when going through problems and situations that they know cannot be solved alone. The word of God is powerful and mighty in our lives if we pray, seek God and listen for His voice as He speaks to us. He wants us to share our problems and our needs to Him because He is our God, He wants to take care of us and bless us because we are his children.

God loves us and He gave His life on the cross for our sins, He is a loving God and if we trust Him, He will save our children and we will live with Him forever in Heaven. We have to turn our children's lives over to Jesus and leave them there because this is the Lord's battle and not ours.

When I lived in Staten Island, New York my teenage son, Tory and my five-year-old son, Jonathan and I would pray every night before we went to bed.

Through your prayers over your children you must declare the Word of God over your children, it counteracts the enemies plans that would seek to destroy or disrupt the lives of our children. One day, during the early morning hour as I was teaching, I was interrupted by a call from the main office and they told me that it was my oldest son, Tory.

He was in distress; someone had broken into our home! This is how good God is, my son usually was down in the basement but for some reason on this day he was in my bedroom, on the third floor with the TV on.

As I was speaking to him over the phone, I told him to pray, stay quiet and don't hang up. As the burglars were ravaging through the house, he remained quiet underneath the bed. Until the police arrived, through our prayers together God kept him safe and protected his life. Through our prayers God hears and answers!

Our children belong to Jesus because they were His before they were ours. He knows their past, their future and their destiny as He will lead them through their journey upon this earth. God told the disciples to let the children come unto him when they wanted the children to leave Jesus alone.

Children are God's heritage and their life was already planned from the beginning of time. Many times our children go in the wrong direction and end up in trouble even death. Our God is always with them in their troubled times.

We don't understand why these things happen to our children but our Father is the author and finisher of their lives and we as parents have to teach our children the message of the gospel and who God is and how much he loves them.

Salvation is the greatest gift man can have in this world. "But thus saith the Lord, Even the captives of the mighty shall be taken away, and the prey of the terrible shall be delivered: for I will contend with him that contented with thee, and I will save thy children. (Isaiah 49:25-26)"[1]

Chapter 5

*R*estoration is coming for our families, to draw them to serve God, to love Him and to love each other. The Lord will give increase and prosperity to our children and our families to carry out His work in the earth if we will obey His word.

"And it shall come to pass afterwards, that I will pour out my spirit upon all flesh: and your sons and daughters shall prophesy, your old men shall dream dreams, and your young men shall see visions: And also upon the servants and upon the handmaids in those days will I pour out my spirit. (Joel 2:28-29)"[1]

God is searching throughout the earth to see who will carry out His will and obey His words and trust in His divine promises.

The family is the foundation of this world and it is a solid structure. And so, the enemy does not like when we come together as a family unit and agree on the word of God.

The enemy becomes afraid us! This is why families spilt up, disagree, become bitter, fall out of love, do not speak to each other, gossip about each other, hate one another and even want to kill each other.

This is a trick from the enemy and families should fight the enemy with the word of God, pray and praise Him in the mist of troubles and confusion. When we seek God and unite together as a family we can win the war of the enemy when he brings attacks against our families. We need to call each family member who has hurt you in the past and forgive them and ask God to heal your heart and theirs too.

God say's in the Bible, "If you don't forgive your brother, sister, your mother and father then He can't forgive you. (Matthew 6:15)"[1] This is a time for families to form a loving relationship again with each other and love on one another.

Chapter 6

*S*ometimes even in the family of God there can be misunderstandings, disappointments or hurts but God does not want that for His children. If any of you have been hurt or disappointed I encourage you to still have bible study in your home, pray and seek God for guidance for your life. More than ever we as the body of Christ need to gather together for prayer in our homes or at your local church.

As we teach the word of God this will help each family member to receive salvation and return back to God and return to the church. As a family we need to do whatever we can to show our loved ones how much we care about them and want the family to function again in a loving manner.

In these times that we live in today we need to fight in faith and prayer for our family members to be saved. When we show our love to one another this will help to bring each other closer. The family is an important part of this world system and an important part of the kingdom of God.

As long as we are separated as a family we are not strong enough to pray and teach our families how to fight the enemy with the word of God. When we pray as a corporate family for this world God will hear our prayers and heal our land. "And it shall come to pass, that whosoever shall call on the name of the Lord shall be delivered. (Joel 2:32)"[1]

Chapter 7

God is restoring our finances and divine increase of prosperity to His people. God is giving us wisdom and knowledge along with His anointing to come upon our mind, our hands as a blessing of prosperity to bless our families and those who are in need. In these days God is sending His angels and they are hearkening His words to prosper His people and give them divine favor.

"And the floors shall be full of wheat, and the fats shall overflow with wine and oil. (Joel 2:24)"[1] This is our Jubilee season and the enemy has to return everything back to us that was stolen from our lives.

As we give back to the Lord, His holy seed and sow into the kingdom of heaven, God will cause the devourer to be rebuked and the windows of heaven to opened unto you. (Malachi 3:10)"[1]

"For in these days, saith God, that his promises to his people will prosper throughout the world."[1] This is our season of no more lack, debt, sickness, disease or bondage! As we prepare and wait patiently on the Lord, He will restore everything that his people has lost. "...Riches and wealth shall be in his house. (Ecclesiastes 5:19)"[1] This is the gift of God!

As we continue to believe God's word and don't give up on ourselves, God will give you divine favor and show you the secrets of His holy kingdom. Everything that we have comes from the Lord, He is in control of everything that concern His children.

In this year 2017 God's supernatural power will overtake His people and do a quick work in their finances and bring glory to Him. Every hindering force over your circumstances will be broken, in Jesus name. God will give you miracles of debt cancellation in your home and in your children's lives.

There is something coming after the pain we have suffered in the year of 2008. There is a breakthrough of supernatural miracles that will speedily over take us into a life of more than enough to help others and bless our families. "Again I say unto you, that two of you shall agree on earth as touching anything that they shall ask, it shall be done for them of my Father which is in heaven. (Matthew 18:19)"[1]

We are the children of the Most High God and we carry the same power as our Father in Heaven, when we speak in authority to our adversaries and we demand what belongs to us, it will be returned to us in Jesus name. As the children of God we must stand firm and not waver in our faith. Always stand strong in your faith and believe the promises of God our Father.

As we obey our Father and follow His instructions, it will lead us in the way He, wants us to go in the year of 2017. "And I will give unto thee the keys of the kingdom of heaven and whatsoever thou shalt loose on earth shall be loosed in heaven. (Matthew 16:19)"[1]

Chapter 8

The blessing of God is being restored in the lives of His people all over the world. He is showing favor and has bestowed great gifts! God is spreading His love all over the world and He wants His children to love one another the same way He loves us and will help us to understand how love can change the lives of many people across the nations of this world.

He wants to bless us to become a blessing to each other. In 2017 it is a year of the harvest! Souls, coming into the kingdom to be saved to the glory of Jesus name. This massive amount of people will show the love of the Father to many in this world and be blessed with the Father's blessing in their lives.

Many people are being restored around the world despite sickness, diseases, struggles, failed marriages, torn-apart families, unsaved children, orphans and homelessness. God's blessing is allowing His people to see that God truly wants to do for many of His children in this season because of the pain this country has suffered as a people over the last nine years.

Through the pain of God's people there comes a breakthrough in the Heavens where the angels are busy carrying out the plans of God in the earth. God has given the angels instructions to bless His people who believe that He is the Son of the living God upon this earth and He will reward His people in their due season.

Our God wants to restore your blessing to you! There are many blessings that are wrapped up for us that has never been opened before. It is time that we open up our gifts that God has for His children. It's time to unwrap your miracle! There is joy in the earth for God's people to enjoy and live the life that He originally had for us since the beginning of time upon this earth.

Now is the time, to collect all of God's gifts in our lives and our families' lives to share and give to one another all across this world. This is the love of our Father to His people all around the world because, we are all God's children and He wants to give us gifts that we have never opened before.

Through all the struggles throughout the years, the breakthrough is here for the people of God. We have to stay strong in our faith and never waver but trust in the Lord. Now is the time, to believe God and His word! His word is misunderstood; dark to the unbeliever, but it is a light to those who believe.

This is the day that all of your possessions that was stolen to be restored to you, in this year 2017 as you enter into the joy of life that God has recovered for you to enter into a year of rest, peace, joy and relaxation. As we sow our seeds in the mist of our struggles and wait on God to deliver us out of all our troubles, He will show you the way!

Chapter 9

*O*ur God is showing the world that miracles are real and He is freely restoring our lives back to wholeness through miracle working power. We need to never forget how God healed and restored people back to good health supernaturally thousands of years ago as He walked the face of this earth.

Jesus can and will heal broken bodies all across the globe to show that He is almighty God and He can heal you too if you believe by faith! Let us not forget that the many miracles that Jesus did many years ago are at reach today. The crowds back in Jesus' day walked for miles just to receive a miracle.

Let us not forget the woman with the issue of blood Twelve years, spent all of her money on Physicians and they could not heal her. When she saw Jesus walking down the street in her neighborhood, she risked her life to get to Jesus for her healing. When she touched the hem of His garment Jesus felt virtue from her.

Of course, there were many that touched his garment but this woman was desperate! When she touched Jesus she was healed immediately, supernaturally by Him. (Mark 5:21-34) Sometimes we have to be desperate for the things that need to be changed in our lives. This is when we need the word to be operated in our lives.

I believe in 2017 Jesus is doing many wonderful works through the hands of His people. Many people all over the world will be looking to see their miracles come forth in their bodies supernaturally and they will!

Many of us are desperate for our miracles to be restored in the lives of our loved ones and friends. So did Jesus!

When He was on this earth, as He traveled from city to city, He was healing people everywhere He went.

If there was a person who was in need of a healing Jesus healed them even when they did not ask.

This is how much Jesus loved us even when we don't show love back to Him.   As the people of God we need to stay in faith and praise our God even in times when we don't feel like it! He sees your hurt, your pain and knows what you need for your life. We don't understand the pressures of life and why we suffer in this world but when we see how our Father suffered on the cross and gave up His life for us we can rejoice that He rose again on the third day.

He suffered for us, His children and sometimes we suffer in Him. Jesus knows our pains and sufferings and He wants to restore our health to carry out His plains in the earth before He returns back to this earth in Jesus name.

Chapter 10

*J*esus is restoring His children's faith! As we live by faith we can believe in those things that we cannot see. This is our faith in God. "Without faith it is impossible to please Him, for he that cometh to God must believe that He is, and that He is a rewarder of those who diligently seek him. (Hebrews 11:6)"[1]

As we seek His face in this New Year 2017, we believe that our faith will grow stronger in the things that we believe God for in our lives. As we enter into this New Year and leave our pass behind us, our faith will lead us into our destiny. As we stay in the word, God our Father will increase our faith in knowledge, wisdom and understanding of how God wants his people to trust Him and leave our troubles in His hands.

As we build our faith in God, He will show us in 2017 that our lives are built on faith through the pure word of God in the Bible. As we read our Bibles this is how our faith will increase and become stronger through the word of God. As the children of God, we need to read with understanding, power and knowledge of the truth.

I believe that this is the year that the enemy cannot steal away your time, strength and energy to keep you from reading your Bibles, attending bible study and attending Sunday services in church. Many people are desperate for a move by God in 2017 in their lives and their families.

As we pray to God we have to show God that we are desperate to see our families be restored in the earth and that the enemy has to return everything back to God's people.

Our faith should be a life style of prayer and seeking God on a daily basis. There is a little saying, "I got up early one morning and rushed right into the day; I had so much to accomplish[2] that I didn't have time to pray. Problems just tumbled about me, and heavier came each task.

Why doesn't God help me? I wondered. He answered, you didn't ask." I wanted to see joy and beauty, but the day toiled on gray and bleak; I wondered why God didn't show me; Why doesn't God help me? I wondered. He answered, you didn't ask." He said, "But you didn't seek." I tried to come into God's presence; I used all my keys at the lock. God gently and lovingly chided, "My child, you didn't knock."

I woke up early this morning, and paused before entering the day; I had so much to accomplish that I had to take time to pray."[1] A lifestyle of prayer is what all of God's people should experience every day! When we wake up in the morning our mind should be on God to honor Him and His word.

If we choose to obey His word and develop a life style of praying and fasting we will see things in our lives change for our good. God wants to restore peace, joy and happiness in our lives each and every day that we wake up in the morning with a smile on our face and love in our hearts for Him.

We are believing that God is restoring faith back in the lives of His people like no other time in the history of this world. As we live by faith through the word of God, faith will come by hearing and hearing the word of God in our lives and our family in this year of 2017.

This is a year that our faith in God will restore what the enemy has stolen from us and our families over the many years.

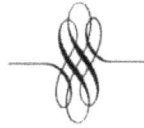

Chapter 11

Our God is sending an abundance of His anointing upon His people, men shall see and God will be glorified. As men, women and children are filled with God's anointing, the power within us will break ever yoke in our lives.

God can wipe these struggles out of our lives in the twinkling of an eye and we will see how lack, debt, pain and suffering have disappeared. He is restoring His anointing back to us so we can carry the same power in us as did rest upon Jesus. I know the Lord will pour out His anointing over His children and they will lack nothing! And they shall be satisfied with their deepest longings and desires in their hearts. When man sees this they will know that the Lord has done this.

As the children of God we need the anointing on our life to break every bondage that has kept us in prison for many years. The anointing will break the chains off of our lives through all the suffering we have went through all our lives. As we walk in the power of the anointing God will use us to carry out His will in the earth!

As we follow the will of our Lord in the year of 2017, He will use us to go out into the highways and the byways to reach the lost, the hurting, the poor and the needy of this world and tell them about Jesus Christ.

God is looking for a people who will take Him at His word and fulfill the calling that He has on your life. This is a season when God will reveal His elected people to go out and carry His anointing throughout the world to spread the gospel in places that has never heard the gospel of Jesus Christ.

God is using His people more now than ever in the history of this nation to reach out and save the lost! If we are willing to obey Jesus commands to do what He has called us to do in this world, He will equip you with His anointing, blessing, resources, finances, favor, strength and power to speak and encourage the lost and the hurting of this world.

He will remove any fear from you and send angels ahead of you to prepare the way for you to go. Jesus is calling His sons and daughters back to Him to praise and worship Him like never before! This is a time of pursuing and calling out to the Lord to reveal His presence in the earth to His people. We are looking for a move from the Lord Jesus Christ in our lives, our families, the church and in the earth. As we call upon the Lord and seek His presence in our lives, He will show up with His anointing and cover us with His Spirit, His power and strength to accomplish the work that He has given us from the foundation of this earth.

Chapter 12

*G*od is restoring the wealth back to His people in the earth. This is the year of our inheritance that the enemy has stolen from God's people. As our wealth is being restored it will make room for evangelism throughout the world. God is raising His people back up to hear His voice and act upon His word and believe the impossible.

Did He not promise in His word that the wealth of the sinner is laid up for the righteous? Yes, the wealth of the unbeliever is coming into your hands. He is pouring out His wealth into the hands of His children who will bring glory to Him.

Yes, He is once again causing the windows of heaven to be open up and I'm pouring out my riches in glory over my children. (Malachi 3:10) God also said, "Yea rather, blessed are they that hear the word of God, and keep it. (Luke11:28)"[3]

The transfer of the wealth will come into your hands as you wait on God's timing. He is bringing all of His benefits and resources with Him for the work of the kingdom. As we wait on God's timing we have to be His servants, to the people who are in need of His presence in this world.

Many people do not know the true story of our Lord Jesus Christ and why He came to this earth to save us from our sins. They need to know why He gave His life on the cross and died and rose again in three days. They need to know how much Jesus loves them and how much He loves His children.

We need to always be ready to serve those who are in need to hear the pure word of God and have the opportunity to learn who God is for yourself. "The wealth of the wicked is laid up for the just. (Proverbs 13:22)"[3]

As the double-fold blessing of wealth comes upon your life believe that only your Father has done this. He is equipping the saints to be ready to receive what was spoken over your life from the foundation of the earth. The release is here now!

We have to listen to God's voice as He speaks to us about our inheritance for the work of the ministry. This transfer of wealth is not about us it is about the salvation of His people in this world.

Now is the time for us to hear the voice of the Lord Jesus Christ for the anointing to be upon our lives as we carry the gospel into all the world. This is the new anointing that will draw people to you through the Holy Spirit as you bring the message of God to people's lives.

When the manifestation of God's Hundred-fold blessing overtakes you, we will give God the highest praise. We will be filled with the power of the anointing that will join us together in faith to be obedience to the call of God on our lives. As we step out into this dark world, the new anointing will bring light to the lost in this hurting world to give people hope again.

Now is the time to join hands together for the manifestation of the wealth transfer into the hands of God's people. "Then Isaac sowed in that land, and received in the same year an hundred-fold: and the Lord blessed him. (Genesis 26:3)"[3]

Chapter 13

Our God is miraculously restoring our double-portion of everything that has been stolen from our lives. This is the year of the double-portion anointing and wealth multiplying back to God's people. What He will do for one, He will do for another if we take him at His word and have faith in Him.

God can only bless what we release into his hands and then trust Him as we sow our tithes. Jesus said and there will be food in my house for my children saith the Lord. God said He will bless us. He will fulfill all His promises to you. (Genesis 26:13-14)"[3] The man became rich, and his wealth continued to grow until he became very wealthy. He had so many flocks and herds and servants that the Philistines envied him.) God had multiplied Isaac and increase him in the land.

When we allow our mind and our heart to be in tune with the mind of Jesus, we become stronger in our faith. As we pray and trust God in the things that we cannot see, then we wait until those things manifest in the spirit and supernaturally become a part of our lives in the natural.

As the seasons change in our lives, the seed that has been planted and rooted in the winter becomes alive in the spring time. Like a farmer he is ready to collect the harvest in his due season and reap the benefits of all his hard work. What we sow we will reap, building the kingdom of God and His holy name in the earth.

Trust God stand firm on His Holy Word and don't waver in your faith. As we continue to act upon the word of God and believe what He says in His word, the promised land, your promise for God's financial anointing and provision will come into your hands. Believe and you shall receive a double portion of everything that you and your family have lost over the many years that you have sown and never received.

God's timing is much different than our timing. He has his own agenda and He doesn't work on our timing only on His timing. As we continue to bless God and help those who are in need of the word, food, clothing, and prayer we can be Jesus' eyes, hands and feet in the earth today to reach out to save the lost the poor and the needy. When we give our time back to God, He gives time back to us. This act of kindness is pleasing to Him as we give to one another.

Chapter 14

*G*od is restoring peace back into the lives of His people and into the world. Our peace has been shaken like it has never been shaken before in the history of this world. Many have lost their peace in this nation.

Our financial institutions in America have affected many families concerning the loss of their homes and their life savings. God is showing His people how to love again and reach out to those that are in need of the many things that they have lost. God says, "The peace that I give you is not like the peace the world gives you."[3]

As God's presence rest upon the people of this world, their peace and joy shall be restored. "And I will dwell among the children of Israel, and will be their God. And they shall know that I am the Lord their God, that brought them forth out of the land of Egypt that I may dwell among them: I am the Lord their God. (Exodus 29:45-46)"[3]

God is raising up people who are not afraid, timid to pray for this country's economy to grow stronger again and be the number one capitol of wealth in America. We need to pray as a country that God will hear our prayers and bless our land once again.

We need men, women, children and grandparents to pray for peace in this nation. God says, "When we are call by His name and humble ourselves and pray, He will heal our land."[3] But, we need to be obedient to His calling!

He will open the heavens and pour out a blessing that we can't even handle and we have to share the blessing with others. He says, "Those that hate you will not enter the kingdom of God, and to leave your adversaries in His hands."[3] God is the God of peace, love, joy and if you don't love your sisters or your brothers than you don't love God.

Jesus said, "Peace I leave you." In the Old Testament it says, "Depart from evil and do good; seek peace, and pursue it. (Psalm 34:14)"[3] When we delight in our Father's word it gives us peace that surpasses our understanding.

As we petition our Father in heaven through our prayers for peace in our lives, our families, our children, and the lives of people all around us, He will hear our prayers and he will answer them in His timing. Jesus didn't forget our cries, He sees and He knows everything that His children are in need of. "I waited patiently for the Lord; and He inclined unto me, and heard my cry. Blessed is He who trusts in the Lord, for God is our savior and he leads us not into temptation, but he delivers us from innumerable evils. (Psalm 40:1)"[3]

As we wait patiently on the Lord, He will bring peace back to this nation. Let us continue to cry out to God for peace in our land, our homes, our schools and our Nation as one under God. "Forsake me not, O Lord: O my God, be not far from me. Make haste to help me, O Lord my salvation. (Psalm 38:21-22)"[3]

Chapter 15

*H*ave you been stuck in situations where you can't see your way out of? The Bible says, "He brought me up also out of a horrible pit, out of the miry clay, and set my feet upon a rock, and established my goings. (Psalm 39:2)"[3] God is building up His people, giving strength from the tough economic times that they have suffered from for the past nine years.

Many people are beginning to pick up the pieces of their lives and rebuild again. This takes strength and endurance to start all over in the building of someone's life. As we pray and trust God in the things we are asking Him for, He will give you strength and power to overcome the enemy and all his tricks. As a country we can pray!

When we pray together as a body of people, God can heal our land and change the hearts of men. God is renewing our strength and giving His people power to fight the enemy with the word of God on their side. "Who satisfies thy mouth with good things; so that thy youth is renewed like the eagle.

The Lord executes righteousness and judgment for all that are oppressed. (Psalm 103:5-6)"[3] In 2017 there is a season of plenty and a harvest that is ripe for the pure word of God to be spoken into the earth.

As our strength is being renewed, the anointing that is upon us will give us the immeasurable power to walk in boldness and have the same mindset as our Father who is in Heaven. As we move out into the valleys, hills and through the utmost part of the world, we go with wisdom, knowledge, power, strength and the garment of praise in our mouth giving God the glory in the earth.

As God is pouring out His anointing upon this earth our children will see the power of the Holy Spirit come upon them. They will preach the gospel to many all across this nation with the word of God in their mouth. God will give them strength, power, wisdom and knowledge to carry out His word all around the earth. They will have no fear but speak with boldness, power and the anointing that breaks the chains of darkness from the lives of their peers. As parents we need to pray and continue teaching our children about God and why He died on the cross for our sins.

"Be of good courage, and He shall strengthen your heart all ye that hope in the Lord. (Psalm 31:24)"[3] This is a season of hope and prosperity for the saints of God! This is the year where all your possessions that were lost must be restored to you."God, your God will restore everything you lost; he'll have compassion on you; he'll come back and pick up the pieces from all the places where you were scattered. (Deuteronomy 30:3)"[3] It is a year for all bondages of sickness and diseases to be broken off your life and your children. Stand strong in the word and don't waver in your faith, trust God He knows everything.

Chapter 16

*O*ur Lord Jesus Christ is restoring our minds with His anointing in the year 2017. We as a people have to make up in our mind who we serve God or man. We have to pray for the renewing of our mind, body and soul to be able to function in this society, living the life that Jesus has already ordained for us.

Or brain and our mind function as one accord, the same as our Father in heaven. We all are one body connected together as one unified with Christ. When you pray, believe that God will give you revelation in the things that are coming upon this world and what we should be doing to bring the body of Christ together as one.

As we pray together we want our minds to be clear of negative forces that try to confuse us with the problems that we are facing. Our enemies are always speaking negative things from our past to keep us worrying, bitter, angry, hurt, unforgiving and many others things. It's time to pray and fast one day at a time once a week from sun up to sun down and tell the devil he can't have our mind or our soul!

There are many other ways we can fast, cutting off the television, hold your calls, stop texting for a day, fasting for an hour or more and pray to the Lord. Find a friend who will do this with you or the whole family. The enemy becomes afraid when the whole family prays together.

"He shall call upon me, and I will answer him, and honor him. With long life will I satisfy Him, and show him my salvation. (Psalm 91:15-16)"[3] When the enemy comes to steal, kill and destroy, we have the right to call upon our Lord Jesus Christ to rescue us in time of trouble. When we call on Jesus, He will always be with us when we are in trouble.

During our prayer time our minds need to be clear of anything that gets in the way of our prayer life and just focus on Jesus and allow Him to speak to us and receive what He tells us to do.

 Our brain and our mind control's the main part of our body. As we go through life's troubles, struggles and disappointments it can weigh heavily on our minds. This is what causes us to focus on the situation and not the word of God. Some of our battles are not ours, they belong to Jesus and we have to allow Him to fight those battles.

When we take on the fight it affects our brain, our mind and our physical body. This type of strain effect's us emotionally and physically in our bodies and takes away our strength, joy and peace of mind. This is the work of the enemy to steal away our peace and our prayer life.

We have to fight the enemy with the word of God in our mouth. When we awake in the morning we need to command our day with the word in our mouth before we even get out of bed. Tell the devil he has no authority over you or your family today or any other day declare it in Jesus name!

As you draw near to God in your prayer time ask God to give you an ear to hear what the Lord is saying and not the enemy. The enemy always speaks to our mind and our emotions.

When you fast and pray you can hear clearer what the Lord is saying to you. Put all your emotion, hurts and disappointments away and only focus on the word and on God. When we practice this method we can gain access into God's spiritual realm in the heavens and He can guide you into the holy of holies just with Him alone. And above all, pray without ceasing!

I hope my book has inspired you to read more of the Bible, to learn God's Word through a spiritual understanding of how it works today. I pray that through the reading of my book whatever challenges you've been facing in your life and in your family that now is the time to come out of those challenges and step into an overwhelming measure of God's blessing and supernatural abundance.

Bibliography

1. Holy Bible KJV

2. God's Creative Power for Healing, Charles Capps, Capps Publishing 1976

3. Holy Bible KJV

Biography

Janice Robinson has been an educator for more than 25 years. She was a teacher in the New York City Department of Education for more than 20 years. Her dedication to the department's After School Programs was recognized by the New York City mayor's office in 1999.

Janice holds associate's degrees in English and History, is a graduate of the College of Staten Island, where she received a bachelor's degree in Education. She continued her education at Columbia University, taking courses in Speech Pathology. She has gone on to further her education at Christian Harfouche Ministries, International Miracle Institute and completed her Master's Degree of Christian Theology and her Doctor's Degree of Christian Theology.

Her work as an educator was also hailed by "Who's Who among American Teachers" in it October 1998 issue. This prestigious Educator award was stated by publisher Paul Krouse". "There is no greater honor a teacher can receive than to be recognized by former students for their excellence and dedication.

Her work as a Reading Specialist was also hailed for her Commitment and Dedication to the New York City Housing Authority Department of Community Operations for after school "Partners in Reading Program on June 21, 1999.

As a volunteer and faithful volunteer, Janice contributes much time and many of her talents to help those in need in her local community of Clermont, FL.   Hope without Faith is Janice's autobiography that focuses on how life lessons can help you master your faith and your intimacy with God.

 No one is perfect and we all make mistakes, but how you allow God to navigate you despite what you see will make the difference between simply surviving and thriving. Janice says, "Teaching has been one of the most enjoyable experiences of my career. As an educator, I want to be an integral part of helping students achieve their success through education."
Born and raised in Montgomery, Ala., Janice moved to Staten Island, N.Y., before finally relocating to Clermont, FL In August 2003. She joined the

teaching staff at Pine Ridge Elementary School in Clermont, teaching kindergarten for seven years.

Janice is a faithful member and prayer intercessor of Faith Point Church in Clermont, FL. Janice continues her ministry to those in need through her church food ministry, Faith Point Church Pantry. And a spiritual leader of Christian Manna Outreach Men and Women of Purpose Inc., a nonprofit corporation.